BLUE

Green Included

S. E. McKenzie

DEDICATION
To everyone who has been left out in the cold

TABLE OF CONTENTS

BLUE

BLUE
I

Blue was just a girl
Who lived in a town
That was sometimes sunny and bright.

There was a rule of order
And hierarchy
Deciding what was wrong and right.

There was a great love of things
All around
While the homeless slept hidden

Outside on the ground.
The atmosphere so thin
Was blue too

During a dark and rainy night
Common Sense was found hanging in a tree.
The shock and sadness

Overwhelmed this little society.
All the great powers to be
Had nothing much to say

BLUE: Green Included

For Common Sense
Depended on trust
Without fear

To grow
Into tomorrow
Without shedding a tear.

And the places where Common Sense had been
Though few and far between
Caused Fear Culture to dread

Words that instigated
Hatred
For Common Sense.

Others said
Common Sense was part of a plot
To take control

Over the External Force's role.
Which was why
Common Sense was shot.

The Authorities
Disclaimed
Such a claim.

Some did admit that Common Sense
And the Downtrodden
Had been forgotten

Which was rotten

Common Sense, Just like True Love
When denied; may have died;
From a broken heart.

Needed a fresh start

True Love knew
That she was the answer too
True Love knew

The girl called Blue
Knew too
That true love

Gave so much to live for.
They say that Common Sense
Always knew too.

BLUE: Green Included

As the days went by
The tune had changed
A story had been arranged.

Some said Common Sense had to die
Even though sadness filled the air
More rumors began to spread

Many were glad and said
The death of Common Sense
Was justified

And called it suicide
Said it was rumored
That Common Sense had died

Through its own hand

Many said they saw Common Sense
Walking down the street
With rope; could not cope.

Such a story was hard to believe
That Common Sense
Would die in such a way

5

For Common Sense did not let emotions rule;
Or allow False Love
To make it look like a fool.

"All over town
So many were kicked down
For their own good," Fear Culture said

"Must be done while still young."

"One's fitness to live free
Must be questioned
By every Authority,"

Legalist said.

II
The tone was hard
Though never thought to be cruel
For order was the rule

Some said False Pride
Of the well to do
Made a target out of Blue too.

BLUE: Green Included

Others said it was the economical
Thing to do
And never a plot defined

To demolish Blue's mind.

So frozen in fear
Blue
Could no longer dream.

Wherever she went
People would scream
In her ear

Leaving Echoes to fear
Dwelling in her head
True Love shed a tear

Outside on the ground.
The atmosphere so thin
Was blue too

During another cold dreary night
True Love came to Blue's bed
And said,

"Blue, I am here for you,
Give good folks
Another try

Common Sense
And Dispositional Attribution
Will one day join again

One day there will be
A better place
Where we will both want to live,"

True Love
Said
"I hope I never die."

And Blue said,
"I do too."
True Love proclaimed,

"There will be a better place
Of my design
Where my name will never be forgotten

BLUE: Green Included

For where there is True Love
Every face
Will be cherished

Where there is no more sorrow
Or abuse of power
Where we will be allowed the time to smell a flower

Without being accused
Nor being abused
Or used."

III

As the years went by
Blue no longer knew how to dream
As fear culture made remembrance

Of the day Common Sense
Was found
Hanging in the tree

Common sense so forgotten
Awoke in pain
To rule again.

THE END

S.E. McKENZIE

GREEN

GREEN

I

Green
Was living his third stage of life
As a happy frog

He often sat on a log
Near the bog
Watching the flies go by.

As a tadpole
He enjoyed living almost like a fish,
But those days are gone.

His log
Gave him a path
To leave the water.

Once his legs had grown;
It was said
That he was a handsome frog

Sitting on a log
Watching the flies
Go by.

II
Green was sitting on his log under the sun
Wondering if this new day
Would be fun.

And there was Boy
Who was watching Green
For Green was the prettiest frog

Boy had ever seen.
And Boy wanted to keep
Green for a pet.

Boy did not understand
That his jar in hand
Would be repressive

Regressive
And could lead to death
For Green.

Boy was not mean;
Boy did not understand
The power of the Tight-Lid-Jar in his hand

BLUE: Green Included

For Tight-Lid-Jar Society
Closed in on some
So a tune was not free and could not come.

And Green's world revolved around the sun;
While a darker world
Was home to more haters

Than innovators;

A world that Green
Had never seen
For he had never been

Trapped in a Tight-Lid-Jar Society.

Boy caught a fly
And gave trapping
Green a try.

But Green was too smart
And knew what it was like
To be free

Never lived life in a Tight-Lid-Jar Society.

So at the speed of light
Green jumped onto a tree
And out of the way and out of sight.

Boy was awed by Green's might
For Green was a little frog
Who could easily fit in Boy's Tight-Lid-Jar.

Green jumped from tree to tree;
For all he wanted to be
Was free.

Boy was as fast as he could be;
With Tight-Lid-Jar in hand,
He ran into foreign land.

The minutes turned into hours
As Green jumped
Over many flowers.

Boy followed Green;
Carrying his Tight-Lid-Jar;
Both Green and Boy had travelled far.

BLUE: Green Included

III

As day turned into night
Boy felt paralyzing fright
For this was his first time

That he had been so alone
Under the stars
So far from home.

So Boy leaned against a log
In the Bog;
A nice place for a frog.

And Boy fell asleep.
Boy's Momma thought the worse;
Hoped Boy was not a victim of someone perverse.

Green was now in a different part of town;
And nothing seemed the same,
His bog, his log

Things that make a home for a frog
Were no longer in sight;
And Green too felt paralyzing fright;

S.E. McKENZIE

As Green awoke in a tree
Girl tried to give Green a kiss
Hoping Green would turn into a prince.

Girl's kiss was a miss
As startled Green
Jumped so high

Even though Green could not fly
All he could see
Was the sky.

He landed on the other side of town.
The side of town
Which was run down

People were rushing here and there
All avoiding eyes
Green had never seen so many feet

Green was hungry and needed something to eat
He saw a fly on a piece of meat
And Green took the opportunity to feast

BLUE: Green Included

At times Green was just another beast
Yanked by the hunger felt by all
Living on the food chain

Made everyone feel so small
When poverty's pull yanked too tight
Men once standing tall, would soon crawl.

Now Green felt so alone;
As all the feet were rushing by;
Green felt homeless and started to cry.

It came too fast for Green to know;
The time which was his to die.
When he was crushed

By all the rushed;
Green's life
Had just gone by.

THE END

The Years Went By

BLUE: Green Included

THE YEARS WENT BY
I

It was just another day
Lou was just a kid
Going to school
In the usual way.

There was a teacher
Smiling in front of the class
She said if they followed the rules
They were all bound to pass.

Lou tried to sit in his seat
But there was something inside him
Causing him heat
Then he landed up on his feet
And he went to his locker to get something to eat.

There was a policeman in the hall
He told Lou that he could make him crawl"
For breaking the rule
And for being in the hall.

So Lou tried to do
What he was told
Though he could not hold
This thought in his mind.

At the end of the day
Lou went home on the bus.
Lou forgot his homework.
Everyone made a fuss.

The teacher stopped smiling at Lou.
She made him stand in the corner
With a dunce cap on his head.
As they laughed at him until he ran away

And hid in his bed for the rest of the day.

II

And the years went by
And what could Lou do
He thought he found love
Like everyone wanted to do.

BLUE: Green Included

III

It is sad but true; Lou's wife did not know to do too.
So she said she was going to leave immediately
If Lou didn't go and see
Dr. Joe Inc. who could have the missing link.

Dr. Joe Inc. looked at Lou in the eye,
And asked him what he did to get by.
He prescribed to Lou a pill with great power
It helped him slow down to smell that flower.

The red one that was called a rose,
But in the middle of the day
The pill's power went away
And the chaos inside Lou arose.

And then everyone
Laughed at Lou
It was true.
So Lou screamed out in his pain

"The pill only lets me be like you
For about four hours so what can I do?"
And then the door was slammed
In Lou's face again.

And the years went by
Until the day the man who counted beans
Was counting the white pills too
And once he was done, he called Lou.

The man said something about the cost
And then Lou felt so lost
Since Lou had no clue
And did not know what else he could do.

Lou knew he would lose the love
He used to get from you
And then the pain it just grew
Lou knew he could never be like you

Lou wasn't sure if it was another lie
Or if it was true that angels were in the sky
Who would be singing a lullaby
To welcome him home, the day Lou chose to die.

As Lou crawled through a tunnel of pain
Lou was surrounded by white light
And as Lou started to fly into the sky
A warhead was passing by.

BLUE: Green Included

And screamed "Turn around, don't die,"

As Lou looked at the warhead
In all its glory
The warhead took another moment
To tell Lou his story

Then the warhead asked Lou
What he could do
"Why was I made to cause so much fright?
So that war does not seem to be so mean and gory?

And I know my power gives fools
Too much might
I don't want to be like this,
Because it is just not right".

And the warhead said
"If I had my way,
I would be making love every day

And then the warhead
Cried when it remembered
The many who died.

And the warhead said
Do you think I want?
To hear them scream?
I have ruined their dream?

And even though their dreams
May have never come true, anyway
I don't want to be the one
To destroy dreams today.

So could you turn around?
And remember,
Take a minute
To land on the ground

Then could you just speak for me Lou
Could you say this in a crowd?
And could you say it real loud
Maybe Earth is Paradise lost

And maybe if you could turn
All their greed and hate around
You would give your love a chance to shine
And maybe you could save your world in time."

THE END

Produced by S.E. McKenzie Productions
First Print Edition June 2015

Enquiries: 1(778)992-2453
Mailing Address:
S. E. McKenzie Productions
168 B 5th St.
Courtenay, BC
V9N 1J4

Email Address:
messidartha@aol.com

http://www.amazon.com/SarahMcKenzie/e/B00H9RWX48/ref=ntt _dp_epwbk_0

www.ingramcontent.com/pod-product-compliance
Lightning Source LLC
Chambersburg PA
CBHW060548030426
42337CB00021B/4487